AN ACCOUNT

OF

The Celebration of American Independence,

AT CLAY LICK, BY THE

LICKING COUNTY PIONEERS.

TOGETHER WITH AN

ADDRESS, BY DR. COULTER,

ON EARLY TIMES IN THE CLAY LICK SETTLEMENTS.

ALSO,

HISTORICAL SKETCHES

OF THE TOWNSHIPS OF

LICKING, BOWLING GREEN, FRANKLIN AND HOPEWELL, &c.

BY

ISAAC SMUCKER.

NEWARK, OHIO:
CLARK & KING, BOOK AND JOB PRINTERS, AMERICAN OFFICE.
1869.

An Account Of The Celebration Of American Independence, At Clay Lick, By The Licking County Pioneers: Together With An Address By Dr. Coulter

Isaac Smucker

In the interest of creating a more extensive selection of rare historical book reprints, we have chosen to reproduce this title even though it may possibly have occasional imperfections such as missing and blurred pages, missing text, poor pictures, markings, dark backgrounds and other reproduction issues beyond our control. Because this work is culturally important, we have made it available as a part of our commitment to protecting, preserving and promoting the world's literature. Thank you for your understanding.

The Pioneers of Licking and Independence Day.

BASKET MEETING AT CLAY LICK.

The meeting of the Pioneers of Licking on Clay Lick, in Franklin township, on Monday last, July 5th, was a glorious occasion. They met in large numbers in the pleasant grove, at Ellis Chapel, near the fine spring at the foot of the hill, where platform and seats had been erected, and there had such a "feast of reason and flow of soul" as is seldom enjoyed in a life time. All were cheerful, joyous, hilarious, but it was all within the limits of becoming mirth—everybody was happy.

The day was beautiful, balmy, delightful—indeed we could not have had a finer day in which to celebrate the anniversary of American Liberty. The occasion presented a scene most emphatically social and fraternal.

The veteran patriarchal pioneer of more than 60 years, Rev. C. Springer, of Muskingum county, performed chaplain services.

Dr. Wilson was President of the day. It is noteworthy that his father, Archibald Wilson, Sr., in 1807 acted in the same capacity at the celebration of independence, in Newark, 62 years ago. Dr. Wilson addressed the meeting as follows:

"Pioneers of Licking County—we have met to-day to celebrate the anniversary of American Liberty. It is a fitting occasion for us to look back and inquire when, and where, this day was first honored by the Pioneers of Licking. During a recent visit to an older brother, George Wilson, who has resided in the State of Illinois for the past 27 years, I received the following account of what he thinks was the first celebration of the 4th of July in this county. He was of sufficient age at the time to recollect many of the particulars. He says it was in the year 1807, and in Newark, on the north side of the Public Square, before the grounds were fully cleared of the forest trees. A dinner for the occasion was prepared by the joint work of the two tavern-keepers at the time, Abram Johnson and Morris A. Newman. The tables were placed in the form of a circle —an abundant supply of meats and other provisions were placed on them—among other things a hog, a sheep, and a deer (the latter having been killed by Hannaniah Pugh.) They were well roasted and placed on the table standing on their feet. The hog had an ear of corn in its mouth, and was trimmed with lettuce. The sheep had a bunch of fennel in its mouth, and was trimmed with parsley. The deer, he thinks, was decorated with leaves, vines, and flowers from the forest. The President of the day was Capt. Archibald Wilson, Sr.—by his side stood the chaplain of the occasion, the Rev. John Emmett, a Methodist preacher, and the reader of the Declaration of Independence, Dr. J. J. Brice. They were in the center of the circle formed by the tables. The orator of the day was to have been Archibald Wilson, Jr., but he having received an injury by a fall from his horse just before, was unable to be present. His oration, in manuscript was read by Dr. Brice. The military were out in force, under the command of Capt. John Spencer. After the dinner and oration were over, many toasts were given, which were responded to by vollies fired by the military. The proceedings of the day closed with a ball in the evening on the hill, in the first house built in Newark. The best feeling prevailed---a goodly number of Revolutionary soldiers were present, who enjoyed it greatly, for they looked upon this day as their political Sabbath. They had assisted in wresting the power to govern the then colonies from the King of Great Britain, and lodged it, as declared on this day to belong, to the people, without distinction. They in this way made short work with the absurd doctrine of the divine right of Kings to rule. Sorrowful will it be when the people of the United States forget to honor the authors of our freedom, or fail to accord to them honor and praise for placing before the world the true principles of government, and the political rights of each individual. Let us to-day, do what we can, as our Pioneer Fathers and Mothers did in 1807, to keep *fresh* in the minds of our people the great *work* that was done on the 4th of July, 1776, by our revolutionary sires."

Dr. Coulter, of Columbus, a native of the "Clay Lick settlement," then read a very interesting paper illustrative of earlytimes—of pioneer manners, customs, peculiarities, and characteristics. Tears came unbidden to many an eye, during the reading of the more tender passages of his excellent paper. The extemporaneous remarks with which he interspersed it, and which were elicited by the presence on the platform of the speaker's school teacher of fifty years ago, (Mr. Samuel B. Hull,) now of Columbus, and of his Christian minister of the same long ago period, (Rev. C. Springer,) who in the early years of his ministry imparted religious instruction to the speaker, were most tender and pathetic, calling into activity the tenderest sensibilities of our nature. His eloquence was of the sort that found the way to the human heart— of the kind that moved our sympathies, and called into action the faculties of our emotional nature.

The acting President of the day, calling another to the chair, after the address of Dr. Coulter, remarked as follows, Capt. M. M. Munson having, by invitation, been seated on the platform:

"Mr. President—I hold in my hand a cane made from a branch of the first apple-tree planted in the soil of Licking, in the year 1800 by Mrs. Isaac Stadden, who at the age of 88, is still with us. She brought the young root, which is all it then was, from Northumberland county, Pennsylvania, and planted it with her own hands. They both yet live—the tree continues to bear its fruit and she protects it in turn. Thus they have lived mutually depending on each other for the last sixty-nine years. Capt. Munson, *you sir*, are a branch of one of the Pioneers of Licking county, and you sir have done much to rescue from oblivion, the very first pioneers of your township, John Jones and wife, by placing their names in the pages of the history of our county. They were the intimate friends of Mrs. Stadden in their early pioneer life in Licking. Please accept the cane as a token of her regard, together with that of Isaac Smucker and myself, for the signal service you have rendered the pioneer cause in Licking county. The cane bears the inscription, "1800–1869. To M. M. Munson, from Mrs. Stadden, J. N. Wilson, and Isaac Smucker."

Capt. Munson responded in substance, as follows, as near as can be recollected:

"Mr. President—You and your co-donors in this handsome gift have effectually surprised me. I have not had the slighest intimation of any intention on your part to bring me before you on this platform as the recipient of this favor. A cane, of course, I did not look for, for you all know that it is an article I do not use, for I am a *young* man, and for proof of that I refer to the ladies in this crowd before me.

"I came here to hear from the Pioneers about the first settlement of this section of our county, and of the incidents connected with early times in the south eastern townships of Licking, and not to take any public part, even the least, in the exercises of this day.

"My friends, accept my thanks for this highly valued gift. I prize it greatly, and I will be more determined than ever before to speak well of the pioneers of Licking, with voice and pen, and defend them, if it ever becomes necessary, even with this cane itself, of which you are the kind donors."

The history of Licking township was then read by the Secretary of the Society; after which an adjournment was had for refreshments. Most persons brought their provisions, it being a basket meeting, but in addition to that an extensive public table loaded with good things, was set in the church, at which many participated, including the soldiers of the war of 1812.

The exercises of the afternoon were introduced by the invocation of the Divine blessing upon the meeting by Rev. C. Springer. A band of stringed instruments, led by Capt. Loughman, furnished music, giving us the national airs and others, such as *Auld Lang Syne*, accompanied by the voice. The accommodating musicians gave us Yankee Doodle,—Tramp, Tramp, Tramp, —The Star Spangled Banner,—Bonaparte Crossing the Rhine,—Hail Columbia and others.

The Secretary read a historical sketch of Bowling Green Township.

Mr. C. B. Giffin read a history of Hopewell Township.

Capt. M. M. Munson read a paper on the early settlement and modern history of Franklin Township.

The two last named papers were prepared by another, and read by the gentlemen named to accommodate their author.

Dr. Coulter, of Columbus, read the Declaration of Independence with much force and effect.

James R. Stanbery followed in some appropriate remarks, in which he gave some of his own early time recollections of events that transpired in the locality of the meeting. He adverted to the time when the late Col. Mathiot and himself practiced law in the justice's courts of Franklin and the region round about. He extended his remarks which were well received, and attracted the attention of the pioneers, who were frequently put into mirthful moods by the speaker.

Mr. S. B. Hull and lady, and Dr. Coulter and daughter of Columbus, were present. Col. Jonathan Hughes, the only survivor of the first family that came into our county, which was in 1798, now a citizen of Washington Township, was with us, too, so also were Mr. Preston, of Chatham, and quite a number from Newark; also from Madison, from Union, Licking, Bowling Green, Hopewell, Granville, and Franklin Townships. Mr. Francis was noticed from Mary Ann, and Mr. Southard from Perry Townships. Mr. Payne, of Brownsville, a soldier of the war of 1812, now 89 years of age, was present, as were many other aged persons of both sexes, including Wm. Brown, of Hopewell, and Nancy Carson, of Newark. The venerable pair who recently celebrated their Golden Wedding, were there too, (Mr. John Coulter and his wife) both far beyond their allotted three score and ten :

"Creep kindly on thou ancient pair,
Whose tottering footsteps downward go,
A few more threads of silver there
  Will make your locks like driven snow ;
But these last years, while death delays,
Are the Indian Summer of your days."

Many others of the old veteran pioneers of Clay Lick and the region round about were there—it was indeed a pleasant occasion to all the "old folks" who were present—one to remember in their declining years. It was a time for the memory to run back to early days—to pioneer times—to the years when we were young—to the balmy spring-time of life, of buoyancy, of energetic, stalwart youth, and to the maturity of a vigorous middle-aged manhood.

But it was not only gray-haired grand sires and grand mothers that graced the occasion, but many in middle-life were there, although the yellow, ripe grain in the field demanded the presence of the reaper. The young and beautiful were present, too, to embellish and complete the picture of sociality and fraternity, which the sylvan scene presented.

Some of the sons of the veteran pioneers present were not there *except in spirit. They could not be there,* for they had gone down in the smoke and darkness and storm of battle—amidst the clashing of gleaming swords, the crossing of clanging bayonets, the crashing of arms, the resoundings of musketry, the roaring of artillery, and of the agonies of their wounded and dying fellow-soldiers.

Others, too, of their no less gallant sons were not there, who had not thus gone down in the shock of battle, but who, like them, had gone forth as patriot soldiers in defence of their government and human freedom. They went forth like the gallant young Shipps, and many others, *but came not back again to participate in our festivities*, after victory perched upon our banners, and bells and cannon and shouts echoed from ocean to ocean, proclaiming the end of the rebellion. They went down no less gloriously, and are none the less entitled to immortal fame, because they were of that ghastly host whose noble lives went slowly out in prison, by starvation, that the nation might banquet in perpetual abundance, and transmit a noble liberty and life to the remotest generations.

It was peculiarly gratifying to all to have the genial pioneer of Muskingum, Rev. C. Springer, with us. Some were within the sound of his voice, while, as the Chaplain of the day, he was invoking Heaven's blessings, that had heard the same voice, similarly employed, in the pulpit and at the altar, *fifty years ago and more.* The Father has kindly lengthened his years; and now, in the evening of life, when age has measurably relieved him from more active duties, it is gratifying to see that his latter days are those of health and comfort, and that honor and happiness attend him in the peaceful quiet of his Muskingum home. With the benedictions of a well-spent life resting upon him, the sun of his *almost octogenarian* earthly career is slowly, but in "marked and religiously elegant splendor," going down happily below the horizon line of a noble life. Few, if any of Ohio's honored pioneers, have lived more useful lives than our venerable patriarchal pioneer the Chaplain, at the celebration of American Independence, at Clay Lick, July 5th, '69, by the Licking Pioneers.

The meeting of the Pioneers closed at 4 o'clock, the venerable Chaplain, after appropriate music, pronouncing the benediction.

    J. N. WILSON, Pres't.
Isaac Smucker, Sec'y.

The Customs, Habits and Characteristics of the Pioneer Settlers of Clay Lick Valley.

BY DR. COULTER.

A few are present, who were among the first pioneers of the neighborhood. They perhaps are the only ones who can fully appreciate first home life, among these hills and valleys. Only those who first cleared off these rough and sterile hills, who erected the first rough cabins, with their clapboard roofs and "puncheon" floors, with blankets and quilts hung up for doors and windows, with chimneys built of split slabs, sticks, and mud, often not higher than a man's head, can now, by contrast, value properly the comforts of a good modern home.

Only those who have grubbed up the thick under-brush and young saplings; who have used the ax in deadening and felling the heavy timber, and the maul and wedge in making the first rails, who have chopped up the trees, piled up the brush, and then been almost smoked blind, while burning the logs and brush, with their fingers and hands bruised and burned, their arms begrimed with smoke and dust, their clothes badly torn and soiled, can have any idea, of the pleasure there is in contemplating a beautiful smooth lawn, without a stump, or a log.

None but those who have first held the plough amidst the roots, stumps, stones, and trees, while the faithful team would be pulling and jerking it along through all these obstacles, can really enjoy that delight, that this same ploughman feels, whilst holding the plough, as it moves smoothly along without a root or stump to obstruct it, while the mellow soil is being turned up to the genial rays of the sun. Only those who have struggled for scanty crops among these clearings and upon the rough and sterile hill sides, the rugged and swampy valleys, can have a proper estimation of the smooth and heavily ladened wheat and corn fields of later years. Only those who have had to convey little sacks of corn on horse back, over winding cow paths, along the sides of the hills, across the ravines and valleys, to the lonely mill, there to wait for his grist, in order that his family might have some hasty pudding for their evening meal, can appreciate the variety of bread and the abundance of bread-material, in our land.

The little boy, less than ten years old, would often, while going up the steep banks, feel his sack slipping from under him, or hanging too heavily on one side; and then he felt desolate enough; and many such calamities these little pioneers had to meet. Mills were sometimes out of the question, and then the hominy mortar would be substituted. This was one of the most primitive articles of the country, and made in the most primitive style. A log about four feet long, square at both ends, and twenty inches in diameter, one end resting on the ground, while upon the other a little fire would be kindled, so as to burn deepest into the center, and in this way a cavity was formed, called a mortar, sufficient to hold a peck or more of corn. Then with a pestle, sometimes made heavy, by the attachment of an iron wedge, the corn would be beaten until the bran or hull came off. This process was assisted by adding a little scalding water, from time to time. After it became thoroughly dry, and the bran was blown away, this hominy, by being well cooked made an excellent substitute for bread.

None but those who were deprived of an education, for the want of a common school system, can see the great benefit of our popular mode of instruction. Our pioneers had no school system, and many of them hardly knew what a school was. The children who now have comfortable school houses, good roads and good teachers, and all provided at the public expense, have but the faintest idea of the desolation and ignorance which prevailed prior to the commencement of our great common school system.

Very unexpectedly I find on the platform with me to day my old school teacher that taught me to read in words of one syllable nearly 50 years ago. Blessings on "thy frosty pow," my venerable friend. You did the best you could for me.

And you, my venerated friend of nearly half a century ago, I had as my religious instructor in this then new country. To you, my friend Springer, and such pioneer preachers, we owe much for your self-sacrificing labors.

May Heavens richest blessings be yours in your declining years.

None but those who have had to raise the flax and prepare it for the spinning wheel, know how to value the luxury of a cotton shirt. None but the pioneer mothers and sisters, who had to spin and weave the flax, and to card, spin, color and weave the wool, and then form their home-made linen and cloth into garments, can appreciate the beauty of a muslindelaine or merino dress. In order to gratify the sense of the beautiful, all their skill and ingenuity were brought into requisition in coloring their yarns and flannels.— Some of us can well remember how one neighbor would vie with another in getting up a beautiful, brown fulled linsey; and then how carefully every good woman, with her blooming daughters, would try to have the prettiest plaids.

How many pictures now come up in the memory, as we review these scenes; the buzzing wheels, the clattering looms, the rattling spool-wheels, the revolving warping bars, are all before me.

Then our cheerful mothers and rosy-cheeked sisters, with energy known only to pioneers, struggling to make their humble homes comfortable and attractive, singing their sweet songs, tripping time to the buzzing wheels, or gracefully throwing their nimble hands to catch the rushing shuttle as it smoothly glides through the gaping warp, with the many-toothed reed rapidly made to thump in the filling threads. As rapidly they follow one another, all bring old home back to view, and we feel that we might be very happy, were we there again.— We might hand in the piece, fill the spools, or turn the quill-wheel, with a better relish than we did then; and not so often ask our mamma to let us run and play a little while.

But there are other persons in the picture. The good old grandmother with serene countenance, seeming often to be lighted up with the reminiscences of earlier years, her foot on the treadle of the little wheel, a bunch of tow in her hand, and a bundle by her side, turning the wheel and drawing out the thread, which will soon be woven into linen for the men's trowsers. Occasionally she stops and calls the attention of her daughter, or some one of the household, who are thumping away with the loom, or buzzing away with the big wheel, and says, 'Fill, is this twisted enough?' or, 'Abby, is this fine enough?' or, 'Polly, is this right?' and when they answer, and she is satisfied, she faithfully works on with the wheel, and the tow passes into thread, until the dear grandmother is tired, and takes her after dinner nap.

More frequently the spinner of tow, was an old girl, who seemed to pass through life with little trouble and less activity. The little wheel turned slowly, and the bunches of tow were not made to disappear very fast; the thread was generally slack-twisted, and when it came to be quilled or woven, it was often remarked that "Polly must have been asleep."

While Sallie occupied one corner spinning, the good grandmother generally had the other, knitting. Sallie was very fond of being warm, and sometimes occupied more than her share of the fire-place, and also of the bed, and children disliked to sleep with her; but she was faithful in her way, and loved her church and class meeting, when her leader did not affront her.

Another intelligent old maiden lady makes a figure in this picture. She was the flax spinner. Her work was well done. She was stately and dignified in manner; a devoted christian of the Presbyterian school; and was quite fond of reading and history. One well remembers her in the group, as having encouraged him to read Pilgrim's Progress, The Holy War, and Josephus' History. These works he read with much delight and profit, and he remembers Nancy Carson as one of the first persons who encouraged in him a taste for reading this kind of literature.

Whilst there were hardships, privations and even wants that the present generation can never realize, our pioneers had joys, delights, romance, and even luxuries, that the present generation can know nothing of.

There is a beauty in living in the midst of wild nature, enjoyed alone by our pioneers. This wild beauty of our country, has gone forever. Cooper understood this well in delineating many of the bright and sterling characters of his works. The old trapper loved the beauty of the wilderness. He loved to be away from the art and cunning of civilized life. The simplicity of wild nature had char..s for him that few people understood. Occasionally we have known persons, who though possessed of much refinement and good sense, still had a yearning for the wild frontiers, who became restive and gloomy under the advance of civilization; who as the rough places were being made smooth, and the wilderness to blossom as the rose, felt a great desire for the primitve forests, and notwithstanding the hardships and privations of their early lives, were willing to encounter them again.

Others again are like the squatter in Cooper's Prairie, whose hand was against every one, and every one's hand against him. Many persons who are unfortunate or vicious, are constantly inclined to pioneer life. The vicious dislike the restraints of society. The unfortunate become unsocial. Most persons however who seek frontier life, the second time, do so in order to better their fortunes. They are willing to endure the hardships without seeing the beauty.

But we said the pioneer had joys unknown to the citizens of old settlements. There is joy in the friendship of pioneer life that old settled neighborhoods know nothing of. In the solitude of the forest, as evening shades thicken around, a few neighbors call. The good dames, neat and tidy seated around the candle, with their knitting or sewing, chat with each other about all domestic affairs, whilst their husbands chat about their prospects, the new settlers that are coming, the rails they have made, the clearing they have commenced and probably indulge in reminiscences of the past, away back in old Virginia or Pennsylvania, mingled with story and anecdote as best suits the times. Now if these social visits were not a feast of reason, they were certainly a flow of soul, very different from the stiff conventional parties of the present day.

Then what pioneer does not remember with delight, the sound of the ax, the clearing away of the timber, the beautiful burning of the brush-heaps "as twilight deepened round us," still and black:

> The great wood climb'd the mountain at our back;
> And on their skirts, where yet the lingering day
> On the shorn greenness of the clearing lay,
> The brown cabin like a bird's nest hung;
> With home-life sounds the desert air was stirred,
> The bleat of sheep along the hill was heard,
> The bucket plashing in the cold sweet well,
> The pasture bars that clattered as they fell;
> Dogs barked, fowls fluttered, cattle lowed; the gate
> Of the barn-yard creaked beneath the merry weight
> Of the sun-brown children, listening while they swing.
> The welcome sound of supper call to hear;
> And down the shadowy lane in tinklings clear
> The pastoral curfew of the cow-bell rung."

The clearing of a rough piece of ground was often made easy in the anticipation of the first crop. Fully two thirds of the land in this part of the county were made to grow tobacco as their first crop. No doubt some here can remember how ambitiously they toiled in cultivating *tobacco*. Each neighbor would try to excel every other in making the best crop. For many years this was about the only produce in this hilly country that brought any money. That man was considered the most fortunate who could have the earliest ripe tobacco, and then still more so if he succeeded in housing and curing it in the finest style. He was sure then to command the market. The man who could first have two or three hogsheads of first rate tobocco ready for the Baltimore teamster, with his big waggon and six big horses was considered the most fortunate man in the neighborhood. Then the returns would be looked for with great anxiety. About the first question to this lucky neighbor on all occasions would be "have you got a return on your tabacco!"

Banking was then in its pioneer condition in this part of the country. But few understood the system of checks and drafts, by which business is now almost universally transacted. Many of these tobacco growers, and especially if they could buy a little to add to their crop, would mount a horse a few days after their team had started on its long and toilsome journey across the Alleghenies—and after overtaking it well and safely on the way, would pass on and reach Baltimore several days in advance and have a merchant ready to purchase when the waggon arrived. Some would take their few hundred dollars in currency and return with it in their pockets. Occasionally horrid tales of high-way robbery would be told, and these individuals would come home with long faces, and the story reported that they had been robbed of every cent. This again was pioneer life—nothing like it now. Instead of four or five weeks for your products to be in Baltimore, twenty-four or thirty-six hours is time enough, for the heaviest articles you have got. A draft or check is sent you, and probably without seeing a cent of money you realize the full value of your crops.

It is impossible for the rising generation, or for the young men and women around us, to realize this contrast. The pioneers alone can do so, and I sometimes think that the transition has been so great, and the new order of things has come on so wonderfully rapid that they almost lose their identity, and can scarcely believe the evidence of their own senses. Those who do realize these wonderful changes, are certainly the most fortunate individuals living. They have revealed to their experience the majestic power and love of the Infinite Providence, beyond any other beings who have ever lived on the face of the earth.

If to experience progress—if to witness the marvellous workings of God, by human instrumentalities, is a blessing, our pioneers are blessed beyond all others. No country has had a transition like this country. All in the old world is tame in comparison.

> Land of the west, though passing brief
> The record of thine age,
> Thou hast a name that darkens all
> On History's wide page.

Our pioneers have seen it all,—have been a part of it, and it is for those who follow after to emulate their virtues, their industry, and to make use of their opportunities to grow wise and good.

Let us who have been a part of this mighty country—who have participated in forming its grand institutions, who have lived to realize that the Declaration of Independence is no *lie*, sing with the great poet Whittier:

> Land of the forest and the rock,
>   Of dark blue lake and mighty river,
> Of mountains reared on high to meek
>   The storm's career and lightning's shock,
>   My own green Land for ever!
> Oh! never may a son of thine,
>   Where'er his wandering feet incline,
>   Forget the sky that bent above
>   His childhood, like a dream of love!

HISTORICAL SKETCH OF LICKING TOWNSHIP.

BY ISAAC SMUCKER.

MOUND BUILDERS WORKS.

The Mound Builders works are found in various parts of Licking township; the stone mound about a mile south of Jacksontown being of the greatest magnitude. It was of gigantic proportions, measuring 183 feet in diameter at its base, and when found by the pioneer settlers was between 30 and 40 feet in hight. Many hundreds of wagon loads of stone were removed from it and used in the construction of the resorvoir and also in cellar walls in the neighborhood, and in the villages along the National road, so that at present it will not probaly average a hight of more than 8 feet.

A tolerably well preserved coffin enclosing a skeleton was found in it some years ago, with a quantity of beads and other trinkets. Other but less authenticated findings or relics are often named in connection with this mound, as the "*decalogue stone*," and perhaps some others that require verification. This mound is situated on high ground, was built of unhammered stone of tolerably uniform size, and very large, and was the largest *stone* mound ever known to the writer. It is the only one of its class in the township. The earth mound on the plank road between Newark and Jacksontown, on the farm of Mr. Taylor, is one of good size, and much interest attaches to it on account of the very careful and scientific examination given it a few years ago, by Professor Marsh of Yale College, and who gave it a very extensive notoriety through Silliman's Journal, as well as in a carefully prepared and well written pamphlet publication. He found in it animal, reptile, bird and human bones—copper beads strung together on fibres whose strands were still perceptible—and other stone, copper and bone implements, rare specimens of the works of our prehistoric inhabitants. The exploration of this mound was more perfect than that of any other within the limits of our county, and its yield of archeological treasure was most generous. G. P. Russel Esqr. of Harvard College, with a number of gentlemen of Newark, assisted in this examination, and retained posession of some of those valuable mound deposits.

There are also several mounds on the lands of Mr. Parr in the vicinity of the great stone mound already described; and one west of the plank road on the farm of J. R. Moore Esq., about two miles south of Newark; also one nearly half a mile east of the Cemetery a mile north of Jacksontown. These are not remarkable for size nor peculiar in any respect, but one on the farm of the late Wm. Bussey at Fairmount is remarkable for size it being 115 feet in diameter at its base, with an altitude, at present of 25 feet. There is also near the banks of the South Fork two miles from Newark on what is called "Cochrans hill," a work or fortification of the Mound Builders. A few acres are enclosed, say between five and ten, with a bank several feet high, thrown out, which made a ditch inside. Fronting the creek where the banks are very steep, there is no ditch for a number of rods. So far as the work was constructed it is an accurate circle.

There is also an earth enclosure of low banks, and small in extent, on the farm of Mr. Ronan half a mile south of the foregoing of about one acre in extent. It has a good size mound standing in the ditch and bank, 30 feet in diameter and 12 feet high.

There is also, on the farm of Mr. J. Sutton, near the northern boundary of the township, a small mound of earth, and also a fort or enclosure of an oblong square enclosing half an acre or more, whose banks have been plowed over and have become almost obliterated. It is situated near "fort spring."

INDIAN HISTORY.

The Indians it is known had a camp in early times on the farm owned by J. R. Moore Esq. and in PIONEER PAPER No. 20, it is stated that there was an Indian encampment in a large sugar grove near the waters of Hog Run, now the property of Mr. Jacob Brownfield, where the indians in early times made sugar. "Big Swamp," or "Two Lakes," sometimes also called by the Indians "Big Lake" and "Little Lake," or what we now call the Reservoir was resorted to by the Indians for the purpose of catching fish. That there was an Indian trail through Licking township and along the reservoir, leading from the mouth of the Wakatommika, (near Dresden) crossing the Licking river at or below the mouth of the Bowling Green Run, to King Beaverstown, near Pickerington or Lithopolis in Fairfied county, about the head waters of the Hock-Hocking is a well authenticated fact; and that the Indians in their journies along this trail sometimes loitered or camped for a time, in Licking township is most probable; and it seems also to be a well established fact that the Wyandots, Delawares, and perhaps the Shawnees had more permanent homes here, than the foregoing remarks indicate. Little that is entirely reliable however, in relation to Indian history, anterior to the settlement of this county by the whites is known with certainty. The foregoing trail is doubtless the one which Christopher Gist and Andrew Montour son of a Seneca Chief, followed in 1750, and it so, Gist was probably the first white man who passed through what is now Licking township. He was exploring in the interest of the "Ohio company," a land company composed in part of Virginia gentlemen, including two brothers of Gen. Washington.

REFUGEE AND UNITED STATES MILITARY LANDS.

In 1801 Congress provided for the survey of 100,000 acres or more of land to be given to those refugees from Canada and Nova Scotia, who attatched themselves to the American cause, during the Revolutionary war, and left their homes or were driven from them, and suffered the loss or confiscation of their property, because they favored the cause of the colonies and took sides against the mother country.

This tract of land extends eastward from the Sciota river forty eight miles into Muskingum county, and is four and one-half miles wide. Two and a half miles of it are in Licking county, extending along its whole Southern border, and two miles of it are in the adjoining counties. A strip of two and a half miles wide of the southern part of Licking township, or about one third of it is Refugee land, and the other two thirds is United States Military or army lands. The 22 ranges of Congress lands adjoin the Refugee tract on the south, in Fairfield and Perry counties, and the two miles or nearly central line through the Refugee tract from west to east forms the northern boundary, of said counties. The United States Military lands, of which two thirds of Licking township is comprised, were surveyed pursuant to authority granted by act of Congress passed June 1st. 1796. The township of Licking except what belongs to the Refugee tract, on the original survey was in the tier of Townships numbered one and in Range twelve.

TIMBER AND SOIL.

The territory now forming Licking township was "well timbered," abounding at its first settlement, in the usual variety and extent of forest trees, the oak, walnut, hickory and sugar or maple being the principal. It was agreeably, and in about equal proportions, diversified by hill and dale—one-third being low, level or flat land, of superior fertility—another third of its area may be called gently undulating, and the remainder is made up of more abrupt and less productive elevations or hills.

The South Fork of Licking, which forms the western boundary of Licking township, and Hog Run, (recently fully described by Judge Brumback,) and its tributaries, Swamp Run, Quarry Run and Dutch Fork are its principal streams. The bottom lands on these streams are among the best in the County—the soil being deep, rich, enduring and exceedingly productive. A portion of the Reservoir is in the southern part of this township, and is described fully in Pioneer Paper No. 85.

ORGANIZATION OF THE TOWNSHIP.

Licking township was organized in 1801, as one of the townships of Fairfield County, and then embraced the whole of the territory (except the Refugee tract) which is now the *County* of Licking, and perhaps a portion of which is now Knox county. Thus it continued until 1807, when it was reduced to half the limits of Licking county, by the formation of the township of Granville. By the formation of Union township on the west, and of Bowling Green on the east, both in 1808, and of Newark township on the north in 1810, and of Franklin township also on the east in 1812, it was reduced to its present limits. The county lines of Fairfield and Perry, which run through the Reservoir, form its southern boundary.

THE FIRST SETTLERS.

Phillip Sutton, John Rathbone, John Gillespie and George Gillespie settled in what is now called Licking township, in 1801. Benjamin Green, Richard Pitzer and John Stadden, located themselves there in 1802, and Major Anthony Pitzer, Jacob Swisher, and Stephen Robinson, and perhaps others, in 1803, *and these were the pioneers of Licking township.*

Mr. Benjamin Green was a veteran pioneer who left his mountain home amidst the Alleghenies, in Western Maryland, in 1799, with a wife and ten children to make a permanent residence for them and himself in the then wilderness country of the North-West Territory. He spent a year near the mouth of the Muskingum, also two years on the Licking bottom below

Newark, on Shawnee Run, on P. N. O'Banon's farm, which he left in 1802 and moved to the Hog Run Valley. In 1822 his wife, with whom he had lived nearly half a century, died, and he sometime thereafter intermarried with the widow of David Lewis, the daughter of Theophilus Rees, who survived him, he dying eight or ten years after the second marriage, at the advanced age of seventy-six years.

In Pioneer paper No. 44, prepared by Judge Brumback, a native of the township, the history and merits of the above named and other pioneers are presented somewhat in detail; I need not therefore here enlarge, but simply refer you for fuller particulars to that excellent paper, which was recently published.

FIRST PREACHER AND CHURCH.

In 1803 Rev. Asa Shinn, then a very young but promising minister of the Methodist Church, was appointed to the Hock-Hocking circuit, then just organized, and which turned out to be one which it took him four weeks to travel over. It led him into what are now the counties of Fairfield, Licking, Muskingum, Coshocton, Knox, Delaware and Franklin. There was upon it but *one* regular appointment within the present limits of Licking county, *and that was at the house, (a good sized double-cabin) of Mr. Benjamin Green, in the Valley of the Hog Run.* Mr. Shinn's appointment, *before* reaching this one, was on the Hock-Hocking River, at or near Lancaster, and the next one after it was at or near the mouth of the Wakkatomeka, or a few miles beyond it at the house of a Mr. Wamsly. Mr. Shinn continued his labors for a year, commencing late in 1803 and ending in the autumn of 1804.

During the year he organized a small society, at the house of Mr. Green, *and this was doubtless the pioneer church in Licking County!*

Mr. Green was a Baptist, and until near the close of his life he occasionally exercised the functions of a minister of that denomination, (and might be properly ranked with the pioneer preachers of Licking county) but he was tolerant of all religions, and as his wife and children were disposed to cherish the Methodist faith, he gave support and encouragement to Mr. Shinn's enterprise. The following are some and perhaps nearly all of the original church members, and those who became such during Mr. Shinn's ministry, to wit: Richard Pitzer, Mrs. Pitzer, Jacob Swisher, Mrs. Swisher, John Stadden, Mrs. Stadden, Sarah Green, and Mrs. Green, the wife of Benjamin Green. It was a sort of a family church, as the male members were all sons-in-law of Mr. Green, and the female members were his wife and daughters; Mr. Green himself was a Baptist, and as already stated, a preacher, but a man of tolerant temper and liberal views. Pioneer preachers like Mr. Shinn—pioneers in religious enterprises like Mr. Green and his compeers above named, and pioneers in the settlement of the wilderness like those of Licking township, were true heroes in the battle of life, and entitled themselves to the gratitude and kind remembrance of the generations that succeeded them, and who entered into the enjoyment of the rich legacies, (the result of many privations and toils) transmitted to them.

The great promise of Mr. Shinn's early career as a Pioneer preacher in the West, was fully realized on reaching the full maturity of his intellect, for he became eminent as an Author no less than as a Divine. It is my deliberate judgment that no man of a better intellect or of a higher order of pulpit talents has ever exercised the functions of a minister of the gospel in Licking county.

His characteristics were well presented in Pioneer paper No. 31, by Rev. C. Springer, to which reference can be had. This little pioneer church, organized by Mr Shinn, in a cabin on Hog Run in 1804, has maintained its existence to the present day, a period of 65 years! The society built a log church in 1818 or a year later, near where Mr. Shinn organized it. This was afterwards moved to the farm of Rev. Benjamin Green, north of where it stood origally; and was sixteen years ago succeeded by a frame building which stands on the farm of Mr. Anthony Pitzer, about two miles from where the original church was built. The pulpit of this church has been occupied with a good degree of regularity through the 65 years of its existence, but the number of its membership is at present rather limited. I give as follows the names of the preachers who succeeded Mr. Shinn until the year 1810, as shown by the conference minutes:

Revs. James Quinn and John Weeks, from 1804 to 1805. James Quinn and Joseph Williams, from 1805 to 1806. John Weeks and James Axly, from 1806 to 1807. Joseph Hays and James King, from 1807 to 1808. Ralph Lotspeitch and Isaac Quinn, from 1808 to 1809. Benjamin Lakin, John Manly and John Johnson, from 1809 to 1810. More than fifty years ago the Revs. James B. Finley and C. Springer, the latter still living, and who is my authority for this statement, held a quarterly meeting in this church. They reached it from the Muskingum region by way of a blind bridle path, which led them mostly through the woods, a little south of Flint Ridge. It is probable that this meeting was held at the time of the dedication of their first church edifice, though not certain. Rev. Noah Fidler, Rev. Jesse Stoneman, and Rev. Levi Shinn, the brother of Asa, were also pioneer preachers here.

THE CHRISTIAN UNION CHURCH.

The Christian Union Church a few years ago organized a society within the bounds of this pioneer Methodist Church, whose members were, for the most part, formerly Methodists, and members of the Hog Run Church. The two societies occupy, jointly, the church edifice, and are of nearly equal strength in membership, neither probably numbering more than twenty or thereabouts. Rev. Benjamin Green generally occupies the pulpit on behalf of the Christian Union Society, and the Methodist Society is served by itinerants, appointed to the circuit.

THE HOG RUN BAPTIST CHURCH.

The Friendship, or as it is commonly called, "The Hog Run Baptist Church," (Old School) is one of the Pioneer churches of Licking township, and of the county. It has had a career of more than fifty-eight years, and has always exerted a degree of influence second to but few churches in our county. Its positive creed, the free, full, outspoken profession of its doctrines, and the unreserved declaration of their belief, by its adherents—their readiness to defend the faith they cherish, and the avowal and prompt support by arguments, of their somewhat peculiar views, as to faith and ecclesiastical usages, have all tended to attract a good degree of public attention. The foregoing considerations, together with the wealth they represent—their numbers—their long history and identification with pioneer times, and other causes, have contributed to make this church *a power*—a church vigorous, widely known, and of considerable influence. The membership of this church has generally been considerable, and crowds usually attend its ministrations. The writer's recollection runs back a third of a century and more when the public services were conducted in an old hewed log church with a gallery running around three sides of it, and when Rev. George Debelt occupied its pulpit. This old log church was built in the year 1818, fifty-one years ago, and was superseded in the year 1860 by a good frame building, which is still occupied. It is a building of good size, and stands on or near the site of the original one, near Van Burentown, where the plank road crosses the north-easterly branch of Hog Run. Rev John W. Patterson was the first, the pioneer preacher of this church. The church members now number 56.

Friendship church was organized Feb. 20th, 1811, by Rev. Thomas Powell and Rev. John W. Patterson. The following persons were the original members: Samuel Meredith, John Simpson, Sarah Patterson, Elizabeth Meredith, Mary Sutton, John W. Patterson, Thomas Deweese, Susannah Sutton, Catherine Deweese, Ann Simpson and Thomas Powell. Rev. Mr. Patterson was the pastor of this church about a dozen years or more after its organization, and was succeeded by Rev. Eli Ashbrook, Elder Hill, Rev. Geo. Debolt, Rev. Christopher Coffman, Rev. Joshua Breese, Rev. John Parker, Rev. Matthew Brown, Rev. S. Meredith, Rev. C. McClellan, Rev. Zachariah Thomas, and Rev. Benj. Lampton, the present pastor, with Rev. S. Meredith associate pastor. Jeremiah Grove is the Clerk, and Mr. George Griffith is Deacon. This society own a Church near Linnville, in which it worships alternately, which was built in 1848.

THE METHODIST AND UNITED BRETHREN CHURCHES IN JACKSONTOWN.

The denominations known as Methodists and United Brethren, have each a frame Church in Jacksontown. They are not large, but may be regarded as prosperous. Each of them is a preaching appointment on a circuit, and its pulpit is supplied mainly by *"itinerants,"* according to the usages of these denominations, respectively.

The edifice occupied by the Methodist Society is neat in appearance and respectable in proportions, and was built thirty years ago or more. That of the United Brethren was originally built by another denomination, and purchased and repaired by its present owners.

The membership of the Methodist Church is 60, with a Sabbath School of 90 pupils, whose Superintendent is Homer Bright.

The number of members in the United Brethren Church is not large, but the number in Sabbath School is 80, Mr. David Kimball is its Superintendent.

THE FAIRMOUNT CHURCH.

The Fairmount Presbyterian Church was organized March 24th, 1834, by Rev. Jonathan Cable, assisted by Rev. W. Wylie and Rev. Jacob Little. The original members were Harvey R. Gilmore, Dr. Joseph Mathers, Samuel Dobbins, Charles Wallace, Mrs. Wallace, James Hamilton, Mrs. Hamilton, Sarah Smith, Harriet Smith, Wm. Bounds, Rebecca Cunningham and Lucy Gilmore. Rev. Jonathan Cable was the first pastor and served from 1834 to 1838.

Rev. Ebenezer Buckingham was their minister from 1838 to 1839.

Rev. C. N. Ransom, was pastor from 1840 to 1846.

Rev. N. C. Coffin, was pastor from 1846 to 1851.

Rev. H. C. McBride, was pastor from 1851 to 1856.

Rev. D. H. Coyner, was pastor from 1856 to 1857.

Rev. H. C. McBride, was pastor from 1857 to 1869.

The present number of members is 63. The number of Sabbath School Scholars, (Mr. Charles Wallace, Superintendent) is 73.

The original Elders were Dr. Mather, A. D. Caldwell, Charles Wallace and H. R. Gilmore. The elders of this Church at present are Messrs Charles Wallace, Jackson Bounds and R. J. Smith. The four following young men, members of this Church, have entered the ministry: Charles Wallace, Jr., Hugh B. Scott, Robert Wiley and (prospectively) J. Conrad. The Fairmount Church, a frame building of fair proportions, was built in 1835. It occupies a beautiful elevation (Fairmount,) on the eastern borders of the township, in full view from the National Road, near Amsterdam, and in the vicinity of a large mound and numerous other works of the mound-builders.

THE FIRST SCHOOL TEACHER.

Mr. Richard Green, whose residence in Licking township, dates back to 1802, informs me that a Mr. Taylor taught the first School in the township, in the Green settlement, about the year 1806. Educational interests have continued to receive a fair share of the patronage and fostering care of the people of Licking township, which is now divided into 8 districts, most of them having a good school house.

PIONEERS.

Col. JOHN STADDEN, was an early settler in Licking township. He came from Pennsylvania to the "Territory North West of the Ohio," during one of the closing years of the last century, as a member of a surveying party, and thus obtained a knowledge of our fine lands. Accordingly he, with his brother, came to the Licking valley in the Spring of 1800, and after erecting a cabin of the most primitive style, a short distance below the junction of the North and South Forks of the Licking, they proceeded to raise a crop of corn. On Christmas day of this year he intermarried with Betsey Green, whose father, Rev. Benjamin Green, had settled upon the Shawnee Run, about a mile below the Stadden cabin, early in 1800, or about the same time the Stadden's came. And this marriage was the first one that ever took place, in civilized life within the territory of Licking county. The late Judge Smith who was then living at the mouth of Licking, and was a territorial magistrate, performed the marriage ceremony. The contracting parties intended the event to have taken place fifteen days earlier, but when Esquire Smith was called upon to ride up the Licking to be master of ceremonies at this pioneer wedding, he signified to Stadden that he would go, if the territorial law which required a notice of all contemplated marriages to be posted up in two public places in the county, had been complied with. This elicited a negative answer from the prospective bridegroom, and as may well be supposed, grated harshly on his exultant feelings. The Squire and the bridegroom however found a way out of the dilemma, which was to stick up the notices, for fifteen days, and this was done promptly, and the delay put the first marriage in our county on Christmas day, in the first year of this century. It has been suggested that the wheels of time moved slowly to the contracting parties during those fifteen days, but Christmas came at length, and the pioneer wedding came off—at least so says Mrs. Isaac Stadden, who was an eye and ear witness, and who I am happy to say still lives. A child was born to these pioneers in 1801, which dying in infancy the same year, was the first death in Licking county.

Col. John Stadden was elected to the office of Sheriff in 1808, being the first one Licking county had. His virtues entitled him to the esteem of his associates.

ALEXANDER HOLDEN, Esq., was an early settler in Licking township, and was a man of more than common capacity, intelligence and scholarship. He was a *Squire* and County Commissioner from 1817 to 1820, and from 1824 to 1827, and was also elected to the Ohio Legislature in 1808, in connection with Knox county, which was the year of the organization of those counties. He was a man of meritorious character, and generally esteemed—was a positive man, one of decision and firmness, and of marked character. He was an honored Pioneer, and died about 40 years ago.

Major ANTHONY PITZER, was also an early settler and rendered valuable military services during the war of 1812. He also secured the public favor to the extent of an election to the office of Associate Judge in 1816, in which he served several years, and to a seat in the Ohio Legislature in 1818 and 1819. He was a man of many excellent qualities, but of limited scholarship and attainments. We have had but few better pioneers, better citizens, better men among us, than Major Pitzer. He was a native of Virginia, and came to Ohio, from Allegheny county, Maryland, in 1803, settled on Hog Run, and died May 14th 1852, aged 86 years.

Isaac Green, Esq., and many other pioneers, natives and emigrants, who were favored by elections to county offices and to seats in both branches of the Legislature are entitled to mention in this connection but I am already a trespasser on your time and patience.

I will only further name Samuel Patterson, Esq., who was elected to the Senate of Ohio in 1848; and Nicholas Shaver, a pioneer settler, who collected the taxes of Licking county from 1820 to 1822. They were both popular and influential.

OHIO CANAL AND NATIONAL ROAD.

The Ohio Canal along the western boundary of the township, and the National Road running through it from east to west, both constructed nearly forty years ago, the former by the State of Ohio, and the latter by the General Government, very largely contributed to the convenience of the people of Licking township, and greatly promoted their material prosperity.

The National Road runs through Licking township from east to west. The work of its survey, location, grubbing, grading, and McAdamizing was accomplished during the interval between the years 1825 and 1835. In one of the earlier years of this period Mr. Thomas Harris, as proprietor of the land, laid out the village of Jacksontown, and named it after Gen. Jackson, the hero of New-Orleans, who was the successful candidate in 1828 as well as 1832, for the office of President of the United States, Mr. Harris being a zealous Jacksonian, especially in the campaign of 1828. His town started off at a lively pace, and soon became a post town of fair promise, but it never attained to a population much exceeding its present number, which is about 270. The different Post Masters in Jacksontown were Jas. Swift, Robert Clark, T. H. Fidler, John Zollinger, R. Stadden, M. Layton, Geo. M. Gray, James Clark, Thomas Detrow and Samuel Gilliand.

Vanburentown is a small village on Hog Run, in this township, 4 miles from Newark.

JUSTICES OF THE PEACE.

Isaac Stadden was the first Justice of the Peace in Licking township, while it was yet a part of Fairfield county. He was elected at an election held at the cabin of Elias Hughes on the Bowling Green, in January 1802; Hughes being at the same time and place elected Captain of the militia.

John Warden became Justice of the Peace a year or two later; and Abraham Wright was next in order and was in office in 1806, and probably some years earlier.

Alexander Holden, Esq., was among the early magistrates of the township, and was frequntly re-elected. Samuel Hupp, Elijah Sutton, John Green, Matthew Black, Herman Caffry, Eldad Cooley, Richard Stadden, John Brumback, Samuel Patterson, Isaac Green, James Pitzer, Thomas Ewing, James Stewart, Jesse R. Moore, B. D. Sanford, Martin Dinsmore, Thomas Germain, John T. Armstrong, John Woolard, Elias Padgett, F. M. Layton and Oliver Davis, were also among the Justices of Licking township, serving pretty much in the order in which they are named.

Among the early settlers of Licking township, in addition to those above named were Isaac, Jehu and Joseph Sutton, Michael and Adam Kite, Samuel Davis, Nicholas Shaver, James Evans, John and Martin Grove, Anthony Geiger, Samuel Moore, John Brumback, Thomas Harris, Thomas Beard, Samuel Parr, Samuel Hupp, Joseph Kelso, Job Rathbone, George Orr, John Hughes, Willis Lake, Derrick Crusen, Samuel Meredith, and others.

THE TOTAL POPULATION OF LICKING TOWNSHIP, WAS

In 1830.................... 859

In 1840.......... 1215
In 1850..................... 1371
In 1860..................... 1296

The following exhibit shows how the vote of Licking township was cast at the four last Presidential elections. In 1856, for James Buchanan, 175, John C. Fremont 59, Millard Filmore 6. In 1860, for Stephen A. Douglas 137, Abraham Lincoln 57, J. C. Breckenridge 56, John Bell, 2. In 1864, for George B. McClellan 216, Abraham Lincoln 42. In 1868, for Horatio Seymour 216, General Grant 48. Total votes were 240, 252—253—264.

The length of this paper precludes any extended remarks upon the character, customs, habits and peculiarities of the Pioneers of Licking township, I must forego the pleasure of doing so, therefore. I conclude with the observation that the majority of the early settlers were Virginians, many of them from the Shenandoah Valley, and that they brought with them and practiced in this their wilderness home, the virtues of industry, frugality, hospitality, neighborly kindness and integrity which so pre-eminently distinguished their progenitors.

HISTORY OF BOWLING GREEN TOWNSHIP.

Bowling Green township was organized in 1808. It is 8 miles long from east to west and 2½ miles wide from north to south, and is wholly. in the Refugee Tract. It is bounded on the south by Perry county, on the north by Hopewell and Franklin townships, on the east by Muskingum county, and on the west by Licking township.

THE MOUND-BUILDERS AND INDIANS

The mound-builders left a few samples of their works within the limits of Bowling Green township, such as the stone mound two miles south-east of Linnville, which is of medium size—and one earth mound near it, both being near the center of the township east and west, which is of good size. There is also one at Amsterdam of no very great dimensions; and one on the farm of Mr. John Hamilton, adjoining Brownsville on the North east, of oblong form, 250 feet in circumference and 15 feet high.

Bowling Green township has no authentic Indian history—it has no legends of primeval times,

When wild in woods the treacherous savage ran,"

but no doubt is entertained that both the mound-builders and our Aboriginal Indian predecessors roamed extensively over it in pre-historic times, and probably had a more or less permanent occupancy of it. The former are traceable by their works, whithin and all around it—works too of gigantic proportions in its near vicinity; and tradition and general belief locate the Red man on all sides of it; indeed that condition of things is known to have existed, by those still living, who in early life were the contempoary of the uncivilized Wyandot, and other nations and tribes who once held undisputed possession here.

FACE OF THE COUNTRY AND PRODUCTS.

Agriculturally and Topographically considered, the township of Bowling Green is properly characterized as *rolling* or somewhat *hilly*, although it has some level or bottom lands, very fertile, particularly along the little streams which flow through it, southwardly, towards Jonathan's Creek, or the Moxahala as the Indians called it, whose tributaries they are. It was originally *well timbered*—the growth being principally oak, hickory and walnut—is generally fertile, producing the cereals and the grasses bountifully, and also corn. There is little if any land in the township that is not cultivable. All the rain that falls in the township flows into the Muskingum river through the Moxahala.

FIRST SETTLEMENT.

The first settlement of Bowling Green township was made in 1802, at what is called the "Little Bowling Green," about a mile south of Linnville, on a tributary of Jonathan's Creek, by some frontiersmen from West Virginia, whose names were Michael Thorn, Frederick Myers, and Henry Neff. John Harris, & Andrew Myers, also Virginians, settled there in 1803, and Wm. Harris, Moses Meeks, Adam and John Myers, and Charles Howard in 1804. The latter was a school teacher by profession and taught the first school in the township. The settlers who succeded the foregoing, after 1804, were Edward Taylor, William Taylor, Joseph Taylor, Jacob Storts, Henry Alexander, John Berry, Joseph McMullin, Rev. Levi Shinn, Nathan Shipps, Elijah Nichols, George Moyer, James Clark, Robert Orr, Landon Warfield, William Chapman, Samuel Parr, Henry Bickell, Alexander McClelland, Walter Roberts, John Weedman, Mr. Mervin, Willis Lake, Sr., Jacob and Adam Brown and John Dickinson.

Mr. William Harris now 77 years of age, was brought to this township in 1804, and though he lived a while in Franklin township, has probably resided more years in Bowling Green than any other person now in it.

Mr. Solomon Myers, who is still living, at the good old age of eighty-one years, was the son of Andrew Myers, one of the immigrants of 1803, and was brought to the "Little Bowling Green" by his father at that time, from near Morgantown, Monongalia county, in Western Virginia, where he was born in 1788. Settlers continued to flock into the township in rapid succession, locating themselves in different neighborhoods, so that when the county was organized in 1808 it was deemed advisable by our county Commissioners to organize the people of these several settlements into a separate township, which was accordingly done, and it was called "Bowling Green." It was the fourth township organized in order of time, and the second after the county was organized, Hanover only preceding it—Licking and Granville being townships of Fairfield county. The little prairie, a mile south of Linnville was called "Little Bowling Green," in contradistinction from the "Bowling Green" on the Licking four miles below Newark, and it gave name to the stream running through it, and has also furnished the name ultimately for the township. Samuel Parr and many others of the settlers who came to this township before 1815 were Pennsylvanians, and most of them from Fayette county.

THE NATIONAL ROAD AND VILLAGES.

The National Road runs through the township of Bowling Green from east to west, along its northern boundary. It was surveyed, located and constructed between the years 1825 and 1833. The towns of Brownsville and Linnville, were laid out soon after the final location of the road, about forty years ago; the former by Adam Brown, who named it after himself, and the latter by Samuel Parr who named it after Adam Linn, who was then about to establish himself there as its first merchant. Brownsville grew rapidly at first, but has been about stationary in these latter years. It is a post town of about 450 inhabitants, O. M. Hamilton being Post Master. Linnville is also a post town, J. Lawrence being Post Master, and has a population of about one hundred.

Amsterdam, half of which is in Bowling Green township, was also brought into existence after the location and during the construction of the National Road. Abraham Boring and George Barnes being its proprietors.

THE PONEY EXPRESS.

The National Road, for twenty years after its completion attracted much travel to it, both of emigrants and general travellers, which gave the villages along it an appearance of considerable life and thrift. Regular lines of daily four horse stages were also run in those days and sometimes they had an additional opposition line, carrying on a very vigorous competition with the regular mail line, which added greatly to the liveliness of the villages on the National Road. A daily "Poney Express line" was also run over the National Road during a portion of the years 1836 and 1837, which for the time being, increased the interest and excitement of the villages through which it ran, and tended to break up the comparative dulness and routine of village life. This *poney express* was established by the Hon. Amos Kendall, who was one of the most energetic and enterprising Post-Master-Generals we have had, for the purpose of carrying valuable letters, drafts, very small packages, and important newspaper slips. Its speed was more than ten miles per hour, being twice that of the mail stage, the schedule time from Zanesville to Columbus (54 miles) being five hours, and the postage on matter carried by it was enormously high. The writer remembers receiving a Newspaper-slip brought by it, containing President Van Buren's inaugural address, in March 1837, which was charged with *seventy-five* cents postage, which by the regular mail would have cost only two cents. The express ponies were rode by boys, and put through on a fast gallop, or a "half run," each one being run about 5 miles. The small saddle-bags which contained the express matter were fastened to the saddle, and at the end of each run the saddle and saddle-bags were instantly transfered from the almost exhausted foaming poney to the fresh one, the rider mounted upon him, and off at full speed without a detention of more than about a minute. The stations in Licking county were Brownsville, Linnville, Etniers, Luray and Etna. Our former fellow-citizen H. S. Manon and a Mr. Jones were the Poney Express contractors from Zanesville to Columbus, and our former fellow-citizen Mr. A. B. Dumm of Newark, then a lad living in Brownsville, rode from Zanesville, to Etniers, near Jacksontown. He informs me that once on an emergency he rode from Zanesville to Columbus in 3 hours and 45 minutes, the rider from Etniers to Columbus being sick. Once, when behind time, he rode from Etniers to Zanesville, (26 miles) in less than an hour and a half. There were five relays of horses on his route. The enterprise proving unprofitable was abandoned in the year 1837.

When rail roads came into use emigrants, travellers and four horse post coaches pretty much abandoned the pike, and the little towns on it became dull and ceased to grow.

THE CHURCHES.

The first religious society organized in Bowling green Township, was effected by the *Methodists* about fifty years ago, at the house of Samuel Parr. Rev's Jesse Stoneman, and Levi Shinn, preached occassionally before the organization of this society, at the house of Mr. James Clarke, who lived in the Southern part of the township, where also a class was formed at an early day.— Rev's Asa Shinn, Robert Manley, Ralph Lotspeitch and James Quinn, are believed to have preached at Mr. Clark's in early times. In 1807, Rev. Jesse Stoneman preached a funeral discourse in Bowling Green, which was probably the first funeral sermon preached in the township. In 1821 the society formed at the house of Mr. Parr, made an effort to build a hewed-log church, which however was never completed, and but little used, if at all, as a church. About the year 1832, this society built a small but neat frame church in Linnville, which, after occupying it a number of years, was sold to the Catholics. In 1839, they built on a lot adjoining Linnville, the frame structure they now occupy. The present membership is about 50, and the Sabbath School, superintended by Mr. S. Tippett, has about the same number of pupils.

THE METHODIST EPISCOPAL CHURCH IN BROWNSVILLE, is one of the earlier societies. It was first organized in 1816, at the residence of the widow Dickinson, one and a half miles north of Brownsville, in Hopewell township, by Rev. James Quinn, where, in 1818, they built a hewed-log church which was occupied until 1830, when the society was transfered to Brownsville, where they built a small brick church. This church was occupied until about 25 years ago, when the society built a large, fine frame edifice, which they still use. The number in society at present, is about sixty-five, and a Sabbath School, under the management of Rev. Mr. Caldwell, of seventy pupils.

THE PROTESTANT METHODIST CHURCH OF BROWNSVILLE, was organized about 1830, and soon thereafter, built a small frame church.— In 1847 the society built a larger and better church edifice which is still occupied. It has very generally been a flourishing and influential church. An excellent Sabbath school of eighty pupils, under the superintendence of Mr. J. S. Griffith, is connected with this church, whose members number about seventy-five, and a flourishing Bible class under the direction of Joseph Hamilton, is also connected with it.

In 1840, or thereabouts, the *Roman Catholics* organized a society in Linnville, and bought the small edifice recently vacated by the Methodist society, who had just completed their new church west of and adjoining the town of Linnville. The Catholic society, after some years, was dissolved, and the church was diverted from sacred to secular uses.

THE PRESBYTERIAN CHURCH in Brownsville, was organized by Rev. W. M. Robinson, in 1845, with eleven members. The present church edifice, a good brick building, was erected in 1846. It has a membership of eighty, and a Sabbath school of eighty-five pupils, under the successful superintendence of Mr. Wm. Black. Robert Hamilton and William Black were the first elders.— Robert Morton and Thomas Black have since been added to the eldership. For further details, reference can be had to Pioneer paper No. 33, written by Rev. H. M. Hervey, who gives many interesting particulars in the history of this church.

There is a BAPTIST CHURCH, about half a mile east of Linnville, which was built in 1848, which is part of, or an appendage to the 'Friendship' or 'Old School Baptist Church at Hog Run,' in Licking township, whose history has been given in connection with said township.

THE UNITED BRETHREN, have a small church in Amsterdam, which stands on the line between the townships of Bowling Green and Franklin. The society is small, many of the former members having united with the society in Jacksontown, but public services are still maintained here.

THE CHRISTIAN UNION denomination, organized a society in 1865, which meets in a school house in Linnville. They have not as yet built a church. The ministers have been Rev's A. S. Biddison, Wm. Henslee, Benjamin Green, and Mr. Underwood. They sustain a Sabbath school and pulpit ministrations with a good degree of regularity.— This church numbers about fifty members, and the Sabbath school seventy, which is superintended by Mr. Isaac Orr. This was the last formed society in the township.— Isaac Orr, James Brown, James Lamp, John P. Switzer, Geo. Clark, and John Dusthimer, were among the original members of this church.

PIONEER PREACHERS OF BOWLING GREEN.

In addition to the Pioneer preachers named, I give Rev's J. W. Patterson, Jacob Young, Chas. Waddle, Mr. McElroy, Abner Goff, Jacob Myers, Joseph Carper, Martin Fate, Mr. McCracken, W. B. Evans, C. Springer, George Brown, George Debolt, James Hooper, Jacob Hooper, Samuel Hamilton, Leroy Swormsted, and J. Gilruth.

JUSTICES OF THE PEACE.

The early-time *Squires* of Bowling Green, were Moses Meeks, Adam Winegardner, John Bartholomew, Alexander Morrison, William Taylor, Charles Bradford, Joseph McMullen, William Armstrong, Sam'l Parr, and Baltus Emory, who served about in the order named. Those of modern times served about as follows: Joseph Hamilton, Joseph Johnson, James Hazelton, T. J. Davis, John Bixler, John F. Bane, James Orr, Adam Linn, N. M. Fisher, A. R. Jordan, F. M. Layton, J. T. Lawrence, James Brown and Isaac Orr.

SCHOOLS.

Bowling Green Township is divided into six school districts, each one having a school house, most of them being good buildings. It is also united with Franklin township in a fractional district.

POST-OFFICES AND POST-MASTERS.

There are two post towns in Bowling Green township, to-wit: Brownsville and Linnville. The post-office in each of them was established nearly forty years ago, and the post-masters were as follows, and about in the order named.

Brownsville post-masters; Joseph Johnson, Moses Brotherlin, John F. Bane, George H. Hood, John Oldham, John F. Bane, (2d term) Alexander Flowers, O. M. Hamilton, Jno. Oldham, (2d term) George L. Buckingham, and O. M. Hamilton, (2d term.)

Linnville post-masters; Adam Linn, William Tracy, William Orr, David Gilland, Thomas Lonon, David Harris, Summerfield Tippett, and Joseph Lawrence.

POPULATION.

The number of inhabitants in Bowling Green township, in 1830, was 1768; in 1840, it was 1464; in 1850, it was 1538; in 1860, it was 1213.

The large population of the township in 1830, was owing to the fact that many families, who were then engaged in the construction of the National Road, had but a *temporary* residence, and were gone when the census of 1840 was taken.

VOTES FOR PRESIDENT.

This township has voted as follows at the last four Presidential elections. In 1856, for Jas. Buchanan, 145; for J. C. Fremont, 106; Millard Filmore, 2. In 1860, Stephen A. Douglas, 138: Abraham Lincoln, 90; J. C. Breckenridge, 15; John Bell, 2. In 1864, George B. McClellan, 147; Abraham Lincoln, 66.— In 1868, Horatio Seymour, 162; General Grant, 80. The totals were 253—245—213—242.

SUCCESSFUL POLITICIANS.

John Yontz and Dr. Walter B. Morris, were among the most conspicuous and influential politicians of Bowling Green Township, and both attained to the distinction of Representatives in the State Legislature; the former in 1835-36-37; and the latter in 1839-40-41. They were not early settlers, and did not remain in the county many years.— The former was identified with the opposition stage interest, which kept up such a lively competition with the regular Neil and Moore Ohio Mail Stage Company, for a length of time, on the National Road. His gentlemanly bearing, fine address, remarkable suavity of manners, affable deportment and attractive presence, made him exceedingly popular, and gave him great power over his fellows He has long been a resident of California. Dr. Morris is a citizen of Missouri, and has been for twenty years or more. Bowling Green township has also furnished a representative in the State Legislature, in the person of William Parr, a native of the township, who has served in that capacity a number of years,

CHARACTERISTICS OF THE PEOPLE.

A good degree of thrift and prosperity, the result of industry and frugality, have marked the history of the people of Bowling Green Tp. Those who support schools and churches as *they* do, could not well fail to reach the average standard, in the practice of the higher virtues and christian graces. The virtues usually developed by life in the wilderness, were practiced to a good degree by the frontiersmen who first settled the township of Bowling Green.

HISTORY OF FRANKLIN TOWNSHIP.

Franklin township abounded in works erected by the mound-builders. Few sections of the Great West, which teems with ancient works are more prolific therein than this township. The mound-builders seem to have had a strong attachment to the region embraced within the present limits of this ancient little realm—this locality and the surrounding country, in which we are to-day celebrating the ninety-third anniversary of American Independence. Their works are such, in numbers and magnitude, all around us, as to warrant the belief here expressed that they greatly out numbered their successors the present occupants.

Among the most elaborate and extensive ancient works found in Franklin township were those on the high hill, which is the most elevated ground in the vicinity, a short distance north of Amsterdam, near to and in a north-easterly direction from Fairmount Church in Licking township. These consisted of a circular wall or embankment, now only a few feet high, enclosing an area of about eight acres. On the outside of this wall is a ditch 8 or 10 feet in width, which was made by throwing the earth out to make the embankment. These works have been plowed over many times and are gradually disappearing. Within this enclosure there stood, towards its centre, and within one hundred feet of each other, three mounds, two being of stone. One of the stone mounds had a diameter at the base of 45 feet, and the other two of 30 feet; and all were about 25 feet high. The two stone mounds were removed many years ago, by Mr. John Cover, who found in the large one some skeletons within three feet of the surface of the ground, which was of persons of very large size. The stone in these mounds were not of large size, and the earth, after their removal, was very black, and gave indications of the presence of fire before and soon after the commencment of the mounds, perhaps upon the first layer of stone or more likely upon altars which had been erected upon which sacrifices were offered as an act of worship, as was the practice of some ancient nations.

By no means the most insignificant of the works of the mound-builders in Franklin township is the large stone mound half a mile south of the centre of the township, on the line between the farms of Messrs. Hoskinson and Irwin. Its diameter at the base was originally about 40 feet, but it is much more now, as an attempt made many years ago, to open it and get down into the middle, resulted in greatly reducing its height, (which was probably about 20 feet,) by throwing the stone around on all sides of it and doubling its original diameter. The earth was never reached in the middle, but its height was reduced to about 10 feet. The late Judge Elnathan Schofield, of Lancaster, who was Government Surveyor during one of the earlier years of the present century, and as such run the section lines here, one of which crossed this mound, made an entry upon his field notes, after designating its locality, and pronounced it a "*singular pile of stone.*" He probably knew but little at that early day, of the works of the mound-builders, particularly of their *stone works*.

Probably the "Tippett mound" has attracted as much attention as any other in Franklin township. It is situated a few hundred yards east of the road from Newark to Linnville and in full view of it, near the former residence of Mr. James Tippett, on the farm now owned by Mr. H. Dusthimer. This mound was 75 feet in diameter and 21 feet high. It was opened several years since and a stone whistle and quite a number of human skeletons were exhumed. Two remarkably well preserved crania were taken out, in connection with skeletons at 20 feet from the top, and just above the level of the land around the base of the mound. The mound was composed of layers of earth, charcoal, ashes and human skeletons. This mound was opened with great care by the Messrs. Tippett, and was one of the most symmetrical and interesting of its class, but I have neither time nor space to go into a more detailed description.

There is a fort of low banks near the center of the township, in part on the farm of P. F. Coulter nearly a mile east of the "Tippett Mound," and about the same distance north easterly from the celebrated Stone mound.

There is also a stone mound near the Madison township line, half a mile or more from Clay Lick; and also one on the farm of A. Inlow, neither of which is of large size. There are also earth mounds of greater or less magnitude on the farms of H. Trout, D. Moore, J. Smith, J. Brownfield, Mr. Handly's "Spring Farm," and also one near the Hopewell township line east of lands of Mr. A. Ballou, besides a very few others not mentioned.

There is but little if any reliable Indian history in any way identified with the territory embraced within Franklin township.

The township of Franklin was composed entirely of United States military lands, sometimes called army lands, and was a part of the extensive tract dedicated by the Government to the payment of the officers and soldiers of the Revolution. Congress by an act passed June 1, 1796, authorized the survey into ranges and townships, of this tract, and Franklin township appears on the plat of the original survey as in the first tier of townships in the eleventh range. The surveys into ranges and townships took place soon after the authority was granted by Congress, and it was to these surveying parties to which Elias Hughes and John Stadden, and perhaps others of our pioneers, were attached. The surveys into smaller tracts than townships, were made at subsequent but not remote periods.

Franklin township is watered by Hog Run, and by Swamp Run, which heads here, and empties into the Hog Run in Licking township; also by Little Clay Lick which heads in Hopewell township and flows through a corner of Franklin; and by Big Clay Lick which has its source near the line between the townships of Hopewell and Franklin, running about five miles through the latter. The bottom lands along these streams are very fertile, and the lands generally, though somewhat hilly, are all productive, there being but little if any waste land in this township. Corn, the cereals and grasses all grow well.

The townships surrounding Franklin, were all settled before it was, except perhaps Hopewell. Madison in 1798, Licking in 1801, Bowling Green in 1802, and Newark, which corners with it, in 1800. The first settlers within the territory which now constitutes Franklin township were George Ernst, John Switzer and Jacob Switzer, who came in the Spring of 1805, the first named from the Shenandoah Valley in Virginia, and the two latter from the "Glades" in Pennsylvania. Mr. John Feasel came in the autumn of the same year, also from the Shenandoah Valley. John Siglar came to Licking township in 1805, from Maryland, and on the first day of March, 1807, he moved into Franklin township. His son, William, then a mere lad, accompanied him, and still lives on the farm upon which his father settled in 1807. In 1808 Mr. John Hull joined the foregoing pioneers, who were further re-enforced in 1809 by Mr. Hugh Scott, Rev. J. W. Patterson, Isaiah Hoskinson, and a Mr. Dustheimer. A Mr. Fulton came, meanwhile, who taught the first school in the township, in a building in the vicinity where we are now presenting these incidents and events of pioneer times. Mrs. Motherspaw, daughter of the pioneer John Feasel, has had the longest residence in this township, (64 years) having been brought here in 1805; and Mr. William Siglar the next longest, (62 years,) or since 1807.

Mr. John Wilkin, Michael Fry, as well as Uriah Hull and a few others, settled in Franklin township in and before the year 1812 when the township was organized, and named in honor of the distinguished American Philosopher, Benjamin Franklin. Isaiah Hoskinson, sr., and Moses Sutton, sr., were elected the first Justices of the Peace, and they were succeeded by Uriah Hull, John Vance, Thomas Cummins, Noah Trout, John Blaney, John Sain, Abraham Burner, Isaiah Hoskinson, jr., Henry Burner, jr., Jacob H. Moore, George Armstrong, Benjamin Brownfield, and George Guttridge.

Franklin township has not now, and never has had a village in it, if we except a fraction of the miniature town of Amsterdam. It has no stores, no grog-shops, no post-offices, no manufactories. The people are almost wholly given to agriculture, and to the quiet, honest, successful pursuit of their avocation, and have attained to a good degree of equality in pecuniary circumstances, and to as comfortable a condition of competency as exists in any portion of our county. The people are sober, industrious, frugal, hospitable, and give no countenance or encouragement to vagabonds, demagogues, busy-bodies in other people's matters, to the idle or lazy, to loafers, vagrants, horse jockies and speculators, grog-shop keepers, professional office-seekers, note-shavers, whisky-drinkers, nor indeed to any who are engaged in such like vicious and demoralizing pursuits. Franklin is literally and pre-eminently a rural township in which the rural virtues prevail. During the sixty years that have elapsed since the first settlement of the township they have had but two county officers, and these were of the smallest. The late Henry Burner was County Commissioner, and Mr. Anthony Pitzer is at present County Surveyor. But Franklin has probably furnished as few representatives for the States' Prison as for the State Legislature.

The National Road runs along the southern boundary of Franklin township, being mainly in Bowling Green, but in several places running a little ways into Franklin, as at Amsterdam and for some distance east of it.

The Flint Ridge slopes off nearly a mile from Hopewell into Franklin township, striking it near the middle of its eastern boundary, and makes that portion of the township, to the extent of a mile in width, unusually hilly, and somewhat mountainous in its aspects and scenery. Little has ever been done, in the way of attempts to turn to practical account the mineral deposits of Franklin township. I call to mind one such effort made about forty years ago, by Mr. Hugh Scott, one of the early and enterprising pioneers of the township, who discovered upon his land a deposit of iron ore, which he mined and marketed; by hauling it to the Granville furnace. It was understood, generally, to have been attended with rather ill success, but whether the enterprise terminated because of the great distance between the ore and the furnace, and consequently, the great expense of getting it to market, or whether the deposit was worked out and the supply ceased, or for other reasons, is not within my knowledge, at present, if it ever was. The mineral wealth of Franklin township, if it has any, may therefore be considered as having been but slightly developed.

Schools were early organized, and in educational matters, Franklin has kept pace with most of her sister townships of Licking county. The township is divided into six school districts, and one fractional one in which it is joined by Bowling Green township. Most or all of them are furnished with a good school building.

The first religious society started in Franklin township was the Methodist Society, which now worships in Ellis chapel. It was organized at the house of John Siglar in 1809, or a year later possibly. The first church edifice they erected was a hewed log building in 1818, on the site of the present building, which superseded it in 1851. The church numbers 36 members, and the sabbath school 65 pupils. Peter Triplett is superintendent. Among the early time preachers who ministered to this society were Ralph Lotspeitch, James Quinn, Jesse Stoneman, Levi Shinn, brother to Asa, Isaac Quinn, David Young, Michael Ellis, Charles Waddle, Rev. Mr. McElroy, Noah Fidlar, Martin Fate, John McMahon, C. Springer, Alexander McCracken, Leroy Swormsted and Jacob Young.

The Lutherans organized the second church in Franklin township.

The Lutheran Church in Franklin township, is the *pioneer* Lutheran Church of Licking county, and the Rev. Andrew Henkle, Rev. Peter Schmucker, Rev. Charles Henkle, and Rev. Amos Bartholomew, were the Pioneer Lutheran Ministers. The first named organized the Lutheran Church in Franklin township in the autumn of 1817, having previously visited and preached to the people in that neighborhood, a few times. They were settlers from the Shenandoah Valley in Virginia, in great part, and had been trained in the Lutheran faith and doctrines. Mr. George Ernst, Mr. Daniel Motherspaw, Mr. John Feasel, Mr. Henry Burner, Mr. Jacob Wilkins, Mr. Jacob Row, the family of John Wilkins, deceased, and a few others, with the families of the foregoing, patronized the enterprise of Mr. Henkle, and soon after the organization of the society, they built a hewed-low structure of small dimensions, which answered the double purpose of a church and school house. Rev. Andrew Henkle's father, (Rev. Paul Henkle) a well known Lutheran minister in the Shenandoah Valley and the successor of the distinguished Rev. Gen. Peter Muhlenberg, of Revolutionary fame and memory, had been the religious instructer of some of these families and of their fathers and mothers.— They therefore readily and joyfully embraced the opportunity presented of having the gospel preached to them statedly, by a minister of their own faith, and that too, by the son of the pastor of their fathers and mothers. Sometime previous Rev. Andrew Henkle had taken charge of the Lutheran Church in Somerset, Perry county, and while living there he, in 1817, organized this church in Franklin township, and immediately thereafter, was elected pastor, and remained such until 1824, when he resigned. It may be remarked in passing, that this early-time preacher, who organized this little church in this then new country, fifty two years ago, is still living at the ripe age of 85 years.

After the resignation of Rev. Andrew Henkle as pastor, the church remained without a settled minister for about two years, but its pulpit was supplied with a good degree of regularity by Rev. Peter Schmucker, of Newark, then engaged in secular pursuits, but who answered calls for ministerial services on the sabbath; and by Rev. Charles Henkle of Somerset, a brother of Andrew, who had at that time charge of some churches in Perry county.

I have stated the fact that the honored pioneers who organized this church in the wilderness were mostly from the Shenandoah Valley, where they and their fathers and mothers received their religious instruction, and which had been imparted to them in part at least, by Rev. Peter Muhlenberg, who was, until 1776, the principal Lutheran minister in said valley, and was moreover, the son of the founder of the Lutheran Church in the United States. In 1776, soon after Lord Dunmore's treachery to the colony of Virginia became manifest, Rev. Peter Muhlenberg, then minister in charge of the Lutheran Church in Woodstock, abandoned his pulpit under circumstances of great interest, which will be detailed hereafter by Dr. Wilson, and took the field as a regimental officer of the Virginia line.

The Rev's Andrew and Charles Henkle, and Peter Schmucker, who were the first ministers to serve this church were also from the same valley, and had been intimately identified there with Lutheranism. Themselves or some near relatives had imparted religious instruction to most of these Lutheran Pioneers, before their emigration to this then new country. The Rev. Paul Henkle, the father of Andrew and Chas. entered the Shenandoah Valley before the close of the last century and preached there many years.—He reached a great age and continued his ministrations in the pulpit to near the close of his life. The writer was one of his audience near fifty years ago, when the venerable minister was far beyond the patriarchal age of three score and ten.—He had a large family of sons, all of whom, I think, entered the Lutheran ministry, in the Shenandoah valley, except one. Those now remembered were David, Paul, Andrew, Charles and Ambrose, making with the father, six in all.

The father of Rev. Peter Schmucker, the other pioneer preacher, who sometimes occupied the pulpit of this church, emigrated to this country and settled in the Shenandoah Valley near the commencement of the present century. Three of his sons, (George, Nicholas and Peter) there entered the Lutheran ministry. Nicholas ministered to the same congregation and from the same pulpit, for a generation at least, which Rev. Peter Muhlenberg had left, when he entered the Revolutionary army.—The two brothers of Nicholas also performed considerable pulpit labors in the different Lutheran churches of the valley. Rev. S. S. Schmucker and his son Rev. S. M. Schmucker, who were son and grand son of George, and Rev. George Schmucker, son of Nicholas, also making six in all, had each charge of Lutheran churches in the valley, which, in the aggregate run through a period of many years. Ministrations by these Shenandoah valley preachers, to these Shenandoah valley christian emigrants, doubtless often brought vivid impressions of old-time religious services to their minds, and could not well have been otherwise than mutally interesting. Their voices, or the voices of those bearing their names had been heard by these people long before, and here they felt that they were not strangers.

In the fall of 1826, Rev. Amos Bartholomew was called to the church as its pastor, and he remained such about 11 years.

After remaining vacant about a year, Rev. J. Manning became the regular pastor, in which capacity he served the church nearly eight years. Meanwhile the congregation had completed the church edifice, commenced during the pastorate of Mr. Bartholomew, and have ever since occupied, which is both neat and commodious.

After remaining vacant about two years Rev. Mr. Richart became pastor, and remained two years. He was succeeded in a short time by Rev. G. W. Shafer, who continued the settled minister several years. After the resignation of Rev. Mr. Shafer the pulpit was supplied for about one year, by Rev. D. F. Phillips, when Rev. William M. Gilbreath received a call to its pastorate, which relation continued two years. He was succeeded by his brother, the present pastor, in 1854, who has therefore sustained the relation of settled minister for a period of fifteen years, being the longest pastorate, by four years, that has been known in the history of this church during the whole period of its existence, of fifty-two years.— This church, now just started upon its second semi-centennial career, enjoys a moderate degree of prosperity, having a membership of almost fifty. It sustains a prayer meeting, and has connected with it a flourishing sabbath school of seventy-five members, under the superintendence of Mr. Harrison Hartman. The members have greatly increased during the long and popular pastorate of the present pastor, Rev. J. L. Gilbreath.

The first elders were Daniel Motherspaw and George Ernst, and those at present in office are Samuel Motherspaw and Alvey Swisher.— Mr. John Motherspaw and Mr. John Orr are the deacons.

The third, last-formed and only other religious society in Franklin Township is the "Christian Union Church." It was organized during the progress of the late rebellion, and was originally composed of those methodists principally who held their membership at "Ellis Chapel," in Franklin, and at "Spencer Chapel" in Hopewell townships, who did not approve of the attitude of the Methodist Episcopal Church on Slavery, the War, and collateral questions, or who disapproved of the introduction of those secular topics into the pulpit. The following are the names of some of those who actively participated in the establishment of this Church. Wm. Henslee Esq., Wm. Rutledge, John Cochran, Mr. Daniel Loughman, Zachariah Rutledge, David Wolf, John Wolf, John Snelling, Samuel Lampton and Wm. D. Rutledge.

They have built a neat, substantial church which stands near the township line, between Franklin and Hopewell. The society numbers sixty or more members and the sabbath school, which is superintended by Mr. John Cochran, has fifty pupils.

Rev's Benjamin Green and W. Henslee have generally occupied the pulpit of this church.

The population of Franklin township in 1830, was 938; in 1840, it was 1131; in 1850, it was 1059; and in 1860, it was 980.

Franklin township voted as follows at the Presidential elections since and including 1856. For James Buchanan, 142; John C. Fremont, 34; Millard Filmore, 5; Total 181.

In 1860, Stephen A. Douglas, 86; A. Lincoln, 39; J. C. Breckenridge, 65; John Bell, 5; Total 195. In

1864, George B. McClellan, 141; A. Lincoln, 33; Total 174. In 1868, Horatio Seymour, 169; Gen. Grant, 39; Total 208.

I close with an incident which, in a few days after my arrival in Licking county, introduced me to the locality, and to some of the inhabitants thereof, of which this paper treats. The camp meeting mentioned was held within about a mile of the spot where we are now celebrating Independence.

In a few days after my arrival here in 1825, I attended a camp meeting held in Franklin township, not far from the large stone mound, some eight miles from Newark.— The meeting was held in a pleasant and somewhat romantic locality, near the western termination of the Flint Ridge. The weather was delightful—the preaching was good, and the surroundings and incidents of the meeting had a flavor of freshness and novelty about them that rendered the occasion one decidedly enjoyable. A slender, tall, erect, long-visaged grave old man, with elongated hair that had passed into the last stage of the silver-grey hue, occupied himself conspicuously as the chief singer of the occasion—the venerable leader in the musical department of the devotional exercises. His name was Siglar I understood, and he sung with spirit, energy, and much power of voice. The great congregation joined him, and they made the welkin ring sonorously, while singing those fine old Methodisn Camp Meeting Hymns. The multitudes gathered for worship from all the regions round about in these ancient groves, were greatly moved, yea! *thrilled* by the inspiring notes of the melodious minstrelsy. The reverberations of those sacred songs, as sung by a thousand voices, in the spirited, natural, unartistic style of our primitive settlers, in those "grand old woods," gave zest to the enjoyment of the interesting occasion, and the scenes and incidents thereof are numbered among the memories to be cherished in the hereafter.

Rev. Zerah H. Coston was the only preacher present whose name I now remember. I had heard him preach a sermon a short time before, in front of the old jail, for the benefit of Peter Dimond, then under sentence of death. I think however, that Judge Fidlar, whom I had heard perform a similar service for Dimond, was also present, though I am not certain. This was my first appearance at a Methodist camp meeting, *but not my last.* I attended one held near Chatham, nearly forty years ago, where I heard Rev. L. L. Hamline preach his celebrated sermon from the text, 'ye are my witnesses saith the Lord.' I had heard him preach it once before, *and it was worth repeating.*— Few men had a more attractive style of pulpit oratory than he. I also attended one on the Flint Ridge, more than thirty five years ago, conducted by our well-known pioneer veteran, the Rev. C. Springer; and another a few years later, held near Elizabethtown, under the same management, at both of which we had interesting preaching. My last camp meeting experience was near Frazeysburg, about two years ago, where I heard two very able sermons delivered by Rev's Philips of Zanesville, and Felton of Columbus. I confess to a partiality by way of variety, for the old style camp meeting oratory—to a strong liking to the *pulpit in the wilderness,* as we had it in days of "auld lang syne."

HISTORY OF HOPEWELL TOWNSHIP.

That the mound-builders once occupied the territory which now forms the township of Hopewell, their still existing works afford ample proof. These works consist of mounds and other earthworks; also of numerous "wells" of various depths, ranging from two to twenty feet. They were doubtless much deeper when first dug, but have gradually filled up, so that many of them are so shallow as to be barely perceptible. It may be observed that doubts exist, in the minds of many, as to whether the mound-builders, or their successors the Indians, dug these holes or wells, but the weight of evidence connects them with the former—the mound-builders were workers, the Indians were not. A great deal of curiosity has been excited as to the objects sought for, by the people who dug these holes; also as to the time *when* it was done, no less than *by whom*. I have expressed my belief that the mound-builders did it; and, that the time of their construction belongs to the pre-historic period of our country, admits of no doubt. As to the purpose of their construction, Mr. Caleb Atwater, who has been regarded as good authority on these subjects, expresses the opinion that they were dug in pursuit of rock crystals and stone arrow and spear heads, which he thinks were in great repute with the mound-builders.

One of the mounds in Hopewell township, is near the eastern boundary line, on the farm of J. J. Van Horn, on the north side of Flint Ridge; and there is one also, well towards the north-west corner of the township, on the farm of Mr. J. Barclay. There is an enclosure or fort of an irregular form, and on both sides of the township line between Hopewell and Franklin. The portion of it in Hopewell township is on the farm of J. Bixler, in the near vicinity of the Great Western Coal Company's possessions. The banks are low, and they enclose two mounds, one on each side of the township line. There is an earth mound on the farm of Shannon Loughman, 150 feet at its base and 10 feet high; also one on the farm of the late George Kregar, 75 feet in diameter, and 15 feet high. There is one also on the farm of William Fisher, and a small stone mound of flint stones on Mr. John Bratton's farm, which was 10 feet high before it was disturbed; besides several others, mostly of small size.

The Flint Ridge which is high ground, about two miles wide, rough, rocky, mountainous in its general features, and abounds in buhr and flint stones. It runs through the middle of Hopewell township from east to west, forming at least one third of it, and slopes off into Muskingum county on the east, and into Franklin township on the west, which it penetrates but a little ways. It forms the summit or highest elevation in the township, the land sloping on one side of it to the north, and on the other to the south. The waters therefore on the north half of the township flow into the Licking, by way of the Clay Lick, Bear Run and Brushy Fork, and on the southern half, by way of several small streams into the Moxahala or Jonathan's Creek. The Flint Ridge abounds in cannel coal, fire clay, and stone-ware clay, but its mineral wealth has been but slightly developed. The buhr stone was extensively manufactured in early times and was found to be a good substitute for the French buhr. The geological and mineral manifestations present some features that to the scientific, possess a good degree of interest. The chestnut and other growths peculiar to mountain regions abound on the Flint Ridge, and the oak, in different varieties, prevails in other portions of Hopewell. The land is of the class regarded as hilly, but it is for the most part productive. No large watercourses are found in Hopewell, yet springs are not rare, and rivulets are coursing their way through all parts of the township.

The township of Hopewell, like Franklin, is in the United States Military tract of 2,500,000, acres, or 4,000 square miles, having the following boundaries: Beginning at the southwest corner of the seven ranges, which is 42 miles west of the Ohio river, in the northern border of Tuscarawas county, thence south fifty miles, to a point in Guernsey county, east of Columbus; thence due west to the Sciota river, at Columbus; thence up said stream to the Greenville treaty line, in Marion county; thence north-easterly, with said line to old fort Laurens on the Tuscarawas river; thence due east to the place of beginning. The first surveys were into range lines five miles apart, and into cross lines five miles apart, called township lines, and these townships of five miles square were then divided into quarter townships of two and a half miles square, or 4,000 acre tracts, or military sections. By subsequent Legislation the undisposed-of portion of this tract was subdivided into 100 acre tracts. The range lines run north and south, and the Township lines east and west. On the plat of the original survey this township is in the first tier of townships, and tenth range. For a few more facts and details in regard to these lands reference can be had to the paper on Franklin township.

Hopewell township was first settled about the year 1805 or 1806.— Wm. Hull, Isaac Farmer, Samuel Pollock, Edward Hersey, John Bartholomew, Jacob Hummell, Thos. Hummell, Timothy Gard, James Glasgow, Isaac Davis, Jno. Charles, George and Samuel B. Hull, Thos. Demoss, George Kreger, Daniel Bowman, Abram Bennett, Samuel Farmer, William Wills, Andrew Livingston, Blois Wright, Alexander, Charles and Zachariah Shaw, Archibald Kelso, and the Gibbons' were early settlers.

Hopewell township was organized in 1814. Isaac Farmer and Samuel Pollock were the first Justices of the Peace, who were elected early in 1815. The former soon resigned, and Edward Hersey succeeded him, and served until 1830, when he resigned. The latter served until 1818, when he was succeeded by William Hull, who served about 20 years.— He was, meanwhile, (in 1827) elected to the State Legislature, in which body he served one year. Esquires Hersey and Hull, were succeeded by James Shaw, Smith T. Price, John Herbert, Samuel Winegardner, Nathan Henslee, P. S. Westbrook, Jas. Beard, Edwin Huff, Stephen R. Tucker, Joseph J. Kelley, Wm. Henslee, W. Chappelear, Abram Hersey and Jacob Loughman.

Gratiot is situated on the National Road immediately on the county line between Muskingum and Licking. It was a post town of about 300 inhabitants one half being in Hopewell township. It was laid out by Adam Smith about 40 years ago, very soon after the permanent location of the National Road, who named it in honor of Gen. Gratiot, then in active service as a regular army officer. It has two churches in it, the Episcopal Methodists and the Protestant Methodists, each having a good building, and enjoying a good degree of prosperity. The former is much the oldest, having been organized in 1830, soon after the town was laid out. The latter has a good church, a large society and Sabbath school, but the building is in Muskingum county.

There is in the immediate vicinity of Gratiot a Baptist church which can, with great propriety be classed with the pioneer churches of Licking county, it having been in operation since 1821, a period of 48 years.

The first *Methodist* society in Hopewell township, as well as the first of any denomination, was organized at the residence of the widow Dickinson, one mile or more north of Brownsville, in the year 1816 by that veteran preacher of the wilderness Rev. James Quinn. The society built a log church in 1818, and as both stoves and money to pay for them were scarce in those days, on the Flint Ridge, they warmed up in winter by burning charcoal in a square wooden box lined with stone and mortar, placed in the church. Rev. J. McMahon, Rev. Martin Fate, Rev. Michael Ellis, Rev. Joseph Carper, Rev. Abner Goff, Rev. James Quinn, and others were the pioneer preachers of this little society. Mr. Landon Warfield was the class leader. The society was transferred to Brownsville in 1829, where they erected a brick church of which mention was made in the paper on Bowling Green township.

The second society organized in this township was in or before the year 1821, half a mile north west from Gratiot. It was of the Baptist denomination, and Rev. Thomas Snelson and Rev. Mr. Caves were among its earliest ministers, and Wm. Baker, Jesse Stith, John Parker, and Daniel Scofield succeeded them. Among its first members were Adam Smith Daniel Drumm, Samuel Winegarner, James Redman, Thomas White, Isaac Smith, Margaret Winegarner, and Henry Claybaugh. The society built a church in 1823, which was superseded by a neat, substantial building that is now occupied. The society is in a flourishing condition, having about 40 members. The original deacons were Adam Smith, and Jas. Redman. Isaac Smith and Dan'l Drumm are deacons at present.

In 1830 Rev. Robert McCracken and others organized an Episcopal Methodist Church in Gratiot, which held its meetings in a school house, until 1836, when they built a good church edifice, which is still used. Lewis Ijams and William Tucker were mainly influential in the first establishment of this society. Rev. Joseph Carper and Rev. Abner Goff were pioneer peachers in this church. The first Sabbath school in Hopewell was organized by this church in 1830, Mr. Lewis Ijams being the Superintendent. It has now, under the Superintendence of Mr. T. S. Armstrong an average attendance of about 70.

In 1832 Rev. Joseph Carper and Rev. Jacob Young organized a Methodist Episcopal Society in the western portion of Hopewell township, with Mr. Samuel B. Hull as its class leader. It erected a church sometime after, and the society now worship in what is known as Spencer Chapel. It has a membership of about 30, and a Sabbath school of 40 pupils, John Keenen being Superintendent.

Rev. Samuel Hamilton, Rev. Robert McCracken, Rev. Martin Fate, Rev. Leroy Swormsted, Rev. James B. Finley, Rev. C. Springer, and others were among the pioneer preachers of this township.

Hopewell is divided into school districts as other townships, and is provided with the usual number of school houses. Mr. Charles Howard, the pioneer school teacher of Bowling Green, also pioneered some professionally in this township, and Joseph Evans and George Hursey were also pioneers in that profession.

The population of Hopewell township was 999 by the census of 1830.

In 1840 it was................1159
In 1850 it was................1227
In 1860 it was................1113
And remains about the same.

The vote for President since, and including 1856, was cast as follows:

1856.
James Buchanan	130
J. C. Fremont	85
Millard Fillmore	10
Total	225

1860.
Stephen A. Douglas	118
Abraham Lincoln	80
John C. Breckenridge	23
John Bell	8
Total	224

1864.
George B. McCellan	139
Abraham Lincoln	36
Total	175

1868
Horatio Seymour	152
General Grant	48
Total	200

The only Post office in Hopewell is at Gratiot. The first Post master was Moses Meek. He was succeeded by Samuel Winegarner, Nathan Henslee, William Sims, S. R. Tucker, F. F. Dutton, L. A. Stevens, William Redman, and the present incumbent Stephen R. Tucker, the second time.

There are two Agricultural Societies in Hopewell, both holding some of their meetings in Gratiot. The "*Gratiot Farmers Club,*" was organized in 1865, and has twenty members. It meets semi-monthly, alternately in Gratiot, and at the house of some member.

The other society, the "*Farmers and Mechanics Association,*" has not been in operation a year yet, but it has about thirty members, and meets monthly in Gratiot. These societies are living institutions—their meetings are well attended—their discussions are lively and spirited—and the impression is general that they are productive of good.

William Hull Esq., and Samuel Winegarner, Esq., can be ranked with the most successful of the politicians of Hopewell township; the former being elected a member of the lower branch of the Legislature in 1827, and the latter to the State Senate in 1846. They were early settlers and men of influence.

NOTE.—The writer does not feel justified in closing these sketches without bringing to view a few of the most aged pioneers of these townships, who have not been mentioned.

MR. T. IVORY resides near Jacksontown, and is over 90 years of age. He has lived in Licking township 40 years, and is now very feeble.

MRS. SUTTON, widow of the late Jehu Sutton, came to Licking county in 1804 and has lived in Licking township, 65 years. She is over 93 years old and very feeble.

MRS. MOTHERSPAW, came to Licking county in 1805, and still lives in Franklin township, where she has had a residence for 64 years. She is between 80 and 90 years old and feeble, but in moderate health.

WM. PAYNE is nearly 90 years of age and vigorous, still able to perform daily labor. He was in the war of 1812, receiving his discharge at Norfolk Va., in which State he was born in 1780.— He has lived here since 1833, and is a resident of Bowling Green township.

SAMUEL MUSSELMAN, of Licking township, was born in Virginia in 1785, and has lived here 55 years. Although nearly 84 years of age, he is in good health.

RICHARD GREEN, of Licking township, is in his 84th year and enjoys a fair share of health and mental vigor.— He came here in 1800, 69 years ago!

SOLOMON MYERS was born in Virginia, and came to Licking county in 1803.— He is now 81 years old, and in full mental vigor and health.

SAM'L B. HULL was born in Virginia, in 1791, and came to Ohio in 1808. He is now 78 years of age and vigorous, mentally and physically. He and Solomon Myers long resided in Hopewell township, but are now citizens of Columbus.

JACOB MYERS, now 77 years old, was born in Virgina, in 1793, and came to Licking in 1801, and has had a residence here 68 years, much of the time in Hopewell township, where he now lives enjoying moderate health. He was a soldier in the war of 1812.

WILLIAM BROWN, of Hopewell township, came from Pennsylvania, in 1818, fifty one years ago, and is now 74 years of age, and enjoys the full strength and health of a vigorous old age.

JAMES HOSKINSON, now 88 years old, and one of the early settlers of Franklin Township, having lived there more than 60 years, is still living, though frail in health.

The Licking Pioneers,

BY GREINER & CO.

THE autumn leaves—how quick they change to purple and to gold,
And each returning season tells that we are growing old;
The frosty handy-work of Time on many a crown appears,
As we so readily behold among the LICKING COUNTY PIONEERS.

The golden dreams of youth are past, yet leave a glorious boon;
A heart that's full of music, with all its strings in tune;
The songs we sung when we were young; the old familiar airs,
Are sweet as music of Æolean harps to the LICKING PIONEERS!

The Indian from his wigwam home, with sly and stealthy tread,
Made many a settlers hair to stand erect upon his head;
The wild beasts of the forest—the wolf, the panther and the bear,
Fell by the deadly rifle's aim, when held by the LICKING PIONEER!

His course, by "blazing of the trees," the daring woodsman knew;
And near the narrow bridle-path, the whirring pheasant flew;
The dead-wood and the under-brush the roaring fire clears,
To make room for the rude log-cabin of the LICKING PIONEERS!

His hunting shirt of buck-skin, his leggins made of leather,
His cap of coon or fox skin, the tail worn like a feather;
A pair of fancy moccasins he kept so nice for Sunday wear—
A lord in the wild, stately forest then, was the LICKING PIONEER!

The feast of pork and hominy stood smoking on the board,
With plates and spoons of pewter, the cup a hollow gourd,
And sauer-krout, pone, fat meat and johnny cake comprised the fare
Of the generous, simple-hearted, brave old LICKING PIONEER!

Then every man his rifle kept, and swung the sturdy ax,
The wife worked in the garden, and in her little patch of flax;
She spun, she wove, she sewed, she knit and plied her household care,
And cheered the manly heart of her brave, stalwart PIONEER!

Her handkerchief about her neck, her cap as white as snow,
She rocked the cradle with one foot, while she spun her flax and tow—
She dressed in linsey-woolsey petticoat—the short gown too she'd wear,
And by kind words and deeds she'd cheer her noble-hearted PIONEER!

Log-rollings, grubbings, raisings, huskings, flax-pullings, quiltings were the style,
And young and old would gather in from many and many a mile,
And mirth, and fun, and frolic, songs and jests, loud laughs and cheers,
Were the order of the day, and night, with the old LICKING PIONEERS!

The young man to his sweetheart then tendered his most gracious bow,
And homeward by the moon's pale light they bashfully would go,
And the beau who'd thus courting go, would breakfast with his dear
In the humble cabin-home of the good old LICKING PIONEER!

This gallant beau and lady fair to church would go, to worship in God's temple,
Where they'd hear of Faith and Hope and Penitence, and of the Life Immortal,
And after church they'd homeward move, indulging hopes, and sometimes fears,
And this was evermore called "courting," by the old LICKING PIONEERS!

These old-time scenes long since have passed, and fellow-feeling's dead;
The call to raisings, rollings, grubbings, huskings, pullings, quiltings is seldom heard—
Good neighborship and the kind deeds of old, now pertain to other spheres,
And not to this, as practiced in early days by LICKING'S GOOD OLD PIONEERS!

Old pilgrims in the race of life,—our journey's nearly o'er,
Our tottering footsteps soon will turn toward the boundless shore,
We're passing through the wilderness of sorrows, hopes and fears,
And soon we'll be "in the land of the leal," with "old LICKING'S" PIONEERS!

We'll soon cross o'er the crystal river, and the city evermore behold,
Whose walls all blaze with jewels—whose streets are paved with gold,
Whose pearly gates are ever open, where all the shining host appears—
And where, through grace, we hope will ever be the home of LICKING'S PIONEERS!

Printed by Libri Plureos GmbH in Hamburg, Germany